# FATHER'S DAY

## BOOKS BY MATTHEW ZAPRUDER

*Father's Day* (Copper Canyon Press, 2019)

*Why Poetry* (Ecco Press / HarperCollins, 2017)

*Sun Bear* (Copper Canyon Press, 2014)

*Come On All You Ghosts* (Copper Canyon Press, 2010)

*Secret Weapon: The Late Poems of Eugen Jebeleanu,* trans. Matthew
    Zapruder and Radu Ioanid (Coffee House Press, 2008)

*The Pajamaist* (Copper Canyon Press, 2006)

*American Linden* (Tupelo Press, 2002)

# FATHER'S DAY
# MATTHEW ZAPRUDER

COPPER CANYON PRESS

PORT TOWNSEND, WASHINGTON

Cover art: Jean-Jacques Prompsy

Copper Canyon Press is in residence at Fort Worden State Park in Port
Townsend, Washington, under the auspices of Centrum. Centrum is a
gathering place for artists and creative thinkers from around the world,
students of all ages and backgrounds, and audiences seeking extraordinary
cultural enrichment.

LIBRARY OF CONGRESS CATALOGING-IN-PUBLICATION DATA
Names: Zapruder, Matthew, 1967– author.
Title: Father's day / Matthew Zapruder.
Description: Port Townsend, Washington : Copper Canyon Press, [2019]
Identifiers: LCCN 2019013490 | ISBN 9781556595783
Classification: LCC PS3626.A67 A6 2019 | DDC 811/.6—dc23
LC record available at https://lccn.loc.gov/2019013490

9 8 7 6 5 4 3 2 FIRST PRINTING

COPPER CANYON PRESS
Post Office Box 271
Port Townsend, Washington 98368

www.coppercanyonpress.org

for Sarah and S., who are my life

# CONTENTS

# FATHER'S DAY

## POEM FOR DOOM

Birds don't lie
they are never lost
above the earth
they never think
*I stole this form*
or *blue is the best*
I listen to it
singing my old man
is far away
singing American
songs stolen
from those who lived
in what now is
but was not
the park which makes
me love him
I am eating an orange
someone grabbed
from nature
over me I hear
controlled mechanical
obsidian dragonflies
search for anarchists
for a long time
I went to school
in the palm of my life
carrying a stone
obeying the law
of semblance
now each night
I bring it back
down to the land

asphodels cover
then I wake
and take my son
out on the porch
to say hello
everything hello
green hills that slept
hello tree
drawn on the side
of a white truck
exorably rumbling
toward some hole
hello magnolia
whose pink
and white blossoms
have left it
for where
oh sweet doom
we are all going
then behind us
we close
the black door
with the golden knob
and sit
in the great
chair morning light
through the shades
always makes
look like a dream
forest throne
all around
our subjects
the shadow trees
rise up

their private thoughts
filling the room
I take them
like an animal
with gentle
ungrateful ceremony
from a leaf
takes dew

## I WAKE UP BEFORE THE MACHINE

I wake up before the machine

made of all the choices

we are together not making

lights up this part of Oakland

it's dark so I can imagine

another grid humming in the east

already people are deciding

it's election day

and I lie in the western

pre-decision darkness and almost

hear that silent voice

saying go down there

the coffee needs you

to place it in the device

its next form will help you remember

daylight is coming

but dreams do not go away

they just move off and change

your mind is a tree

on a little hill

surrounded by grasses

that look up and say

father wind

loves moving through you

## DECEMBER

At first we all
went down to the lake
to hold hands,
all the multicolored
signs said
with love
we will resist,
over my head
I lifted my son
so he could see
what people
look like
when they hear
the song Imagine,
a few weeks later
again people stood
at the water,
this time at night
holding flashlights
to say to fire
you came
without permission
and took our young
gentle soldiers
for art
so we will show
even with our old
technology
we can see
each other
without you,
others booed

the mayor which was
my friend said
*understandable,*
I don't know
what is anymore,
everyone understands
in a different
contradictory way
the so far purely
abstract
catastrophe
so many millions
of choices
brought us,
not too far
from the water
I sat on the couch
below the sound
of blades
drinking amber
numbing fluid
my thoughts
chopping the air
feeling not
what is the word
to be a father
*equipped,*
mine never told me
where to hide
a brick of gold,
for a long time
I have known
no voices
will come at last

to tell us how
to stop pretending
we don't know
if it is not
safe for some
it is not
for anyone.

## MY LIFE

four years ago
on Martin Luther King Day
in the afternoon
the little strip
said it was time,
so we did it twice
laughing through
that grim comical
despair familiar
to all modern
conceivers,
it was magical
only that it worked
but now I know
it was then
my life began,
we made so
many plans
circumstances
already waited
to obviate,
suddenly he was born,
a room full of blood
and shouting,
he stayed calm
sleeping on my chest
a long time while
they sewed you up,
he and I
in a room alone
under a soft white light,
one nurse came

to say it was all right,
you were not
but you were there,
I talked to him,
whatever I said
I don't remember,
then came the proud
sleepless happy
sorrow months
then slow realizing
playground dread,
the year
of diagnosis when
our life kept
being a place
for worsening fears
in enviable comfort
to occur as we
graciously received
the humiliation
of being the ones
gratefully not to be,
those many hours
in the bedroom screaming
then lurching out
for exhausted walks,
trying with no
success to protect
us from everything
anyone could say,
gradually all our friends
and family lovingly
without intention
back into their lives

abandoned us,
we did not know
it was just us
growing stronger
in relation to a future
where no one
without permission
may join us,
now we're moving
fortunate ones
from our beloved house
to another on a hill
near a school
where his mind
happily alive
in music can grow,
can I say he is
my painful joy,
he thinks
in rhyme,
the truest friend
to no one yet
he is my
favorite word
remembrancer,
why am I telling you
you know it all
and yet to say
my version
of our story
in the morning
very early
imagining you
sitting behind me

touching my shoulder
scares and
comforts me,
before I go
I want to tell you
something new,
all the time
I walk around
thinking this life
yes but is this lovely
accident correct
and someday
how will it happen
to our bodies
and when it does
will we feel
like we lived
or just lived through

## I MET MY WIFE

I met my wife
in a bar
you could throw
a Frisbee from
and hit Emily
Dickinson's grave
which would be
uncool and not.
Until that night
my whole life
had been a conference
where voices
amiably disagreed
until paralysis ensued.
When I looked
in her face
something actually
for the first time
spoke saying
Home is where
you've never lived,
not yet.
What else.
Before she said it
I knew her Old
Testament name.
Home as everyone
knows is hard,
in each room
the most terrible
moments keep
lasting, obscure

green velvet
continual past
light from under
every doorway
pours into
the hallway,
you are drawn
to enter and fear.
It's horrible
and good to go
through each door
into every room,
to keep standing
in that green light,
to spread your arms
and take it
into your fur,
no fantasy
is ever better,
still alive you
open your eyes
and go back down
the stairs to find
the other
in the kitchen
stirring something,
someone says
have a cookie,
it won't kill you.

## GRADUATION DAY

Drawn by ceremonial obligation
up from sleep I woke and stepped
into the borrowed black robes
all ghost bureaucrats trained
to redirect dreaming pretend
we do not like to wear. I drove
my black car to the stadium
to sit on stage and be watched
watching young expectant spirits
one by one with dread certainty
pass before me, clouded
in their names. Then listened
to no one in their speeches say
you're welcome for allowing
us not to tell you it's already
too late to learn anything
or defend whatever accidental
instrument in us causes
all these useless thoughts.
Like if you walked for hours
through the vast black avenues
of those server farms all of us
with our endless attention built,
you could almost feel the same
peaceful disinterest as when
your parents talking and smoking
raised their heads for a moment
to smile and tell you go back
upstairs and read the book
you love about myths that explain
weather and death. Now it is
almost June and they are finally

the children they always were.
So more precise than anyone
has ever had to be, go forget
everything we told you
so you can fix what we kept
destroying by calling the future.

## TODAY

Justice Kennedy retired
farewell pious blowhard
from the dark collective
grief of half of us I stole
one long hour to think
despair is a privilege
we can't afford but really
a few of us totally can
which is of course precisely
what creates the vacuum
this continual impervious
self-satisfied classic righteous
American malice can gleefully
pour into to crush
everything especially
our clever laments
today all my rich white
friends are talking again
about leaving for houses
they have not yet decided
to purchase over the border
it's grotesque yet I too
admit when we finally
realized our son who
remembers every song
would not speak like
all the others
moving deeper into
places we could not go
we without hesitation
in fear with our money
went over whatever

we thought separated us
from a solution to this
and also other problems
most don't even get to name
today in my hybrid
I too see the blue tarps
under the freeway as I drive
him to another appointment
he has the softest skin
and is never frantic
he loves when the trucks get
so dangerously close
and sings the same song
I taught him years ago
when I was in despair
about how to be happy
it's been so much better
but still I walk around
as if something that cannot
fail protects everything I need
and only now can I ask
what dream was I born into
and what will happen
when the dreamer wakes

## FATHER'S DAY

yesterday we walked
down to the park
the worn one
our dear city
tries to maintain
next to the library
a flash of terror
my kid ran through
people playing soccer
to the swings
I talked to some dads
nice business guys
with the usual
deep sorrow wells
I recognize
from the mirror
their eyes were wild
we're all waiting
with dread
for father's day
we don't deserve
a little brunch
followed by
a sleepy blow job
we all know
merely to survive
this totally
survivable life
is not enough
what good will it do
we must not think
this is some dream

the children sleeping
alone in some
detention center
don't need
our brilliant sincerity
it's not enough
to give some money
make some calls
they are not ours
but they are
we are the first
new fathers
ours failed
where we cannot
stop waiting
there are no others

## WHEN I WAS FIFTEEN

When I was fifteen
I suddenly knew
I would never
understand geometry.
Who was my teacher?
That name is gone.
I only remember
the gray feeling
in a classroom
filled with vast
theoretical distances.
I can still see
odd shapes
drawn on the board,
and those inscrutable
formulas everyone
was busily into
their notebooks scribbling.
I looked down
at the Velcro
straps of my entirely
white shoes and knew
inside me things
had long ago gone
terribly wrong
and would continue
to be. When
the field hockey star
broke her knee,
I wrote a story
for the school paper
then brought her

the history notes
in the snow.
She stood
in the threshold,
a whole firelit life
of mysterious
familial warmth
glowing behind her,
and took them
from my hands
like the blameless
queen of elegant
violence she was.
Walking home
encased in immense
amounts of down
I listened to
the analog ghost
in the machine
pour from the cassette
I had drawn
flowers on.
Into my ears
it sang everything
they told you
makes you believe
you are trapped
in a snow globe
forgotten in a dark
closet where exhausted
shadows argue
what is sorrow
cannot become joy,
but I am here

from the future
to tell you
you are not,
all you must do
is stay asleep
a few more years,
great traveler waiting to go.

## PAUL RYAN

Paul Ryan
your name so
perfectly
combines
New Testament
righteous purity
with American
white immigrant
self-pity
it must have
been invented
in some brushed
metallic building
the exact color
of despair
you could
walk right past
and never see
where sad
ghosts
think all day
about the most
efficient way
to eat light
they know
we need it
it could be used
to power
every black box
every machine
the ghosts
don't want

to eat the light
but they must
they work
for immense demons
Paul Ryan
you do too
many years ago
they filled you
with the carefully
harvested breath
of emptied factories
then grew
your house
its pretend love
and grim commotion
and the slow
imperceptible
drip of ideology
contaminated
your blood until
you actually
thought
your struggles
and success
were real
so your job
was to put
on your red
hat and go
into the world
to tell us what is
is by nature
just and only vast
forces are real

and even a slight
compassion flicker
is just a selfish
desire to seem
unselfish
and maybe you're right
there can be
no more
pure water
we are defeated
and must
accept immortal
drought
but I don't know
it seems to me
the dark triumph
that animates
your tragic corpse
drinks hate
so I will not
drink it
Paul Ryan
I love you
I kiss
your dry lips
to defeat you

## OUR CUSTODY

This year was serious
in a dumb way,
and hilarious
like a grave cut
into a smile.
Dreams constantly
died without names.
We listened to the earth
say nothing, and knew
everything.
The earth a grave
we throw words into.
Seeds in a dark
arctic closet
wait for the new garden
tended by machines.
One whose name
will become dust said
in the shadow
under an umbrella
in our custody
only two died,
so it was a good year.
What can we say?
They were children
and will always be.

## POEM FOR PASSENGERS

Like all strangers who temporarily
find themselves moving in the same direction
we look out the window
without really seeing or down at our phones
trying to catch the dying signal
then the famous lonesome whistle
so many singers have sung about
blows and our bodies shudder
soon we will pick up speed
and pass the abandoned factories
there has lately been so much conversation about
through broken windows they stare
asking us to decide
but we fall asleep next to each other
riding into the tunnel
sharing without knowing the same dream
in it we are carrying something
an empty casket somehow so heavy
only together can we carry it
over a bridge in the snow
emerging suddenly into the light
we wake and open our laptops
or a book about murder
or a glossy magazine
though we are mostly awake
part of us still goes on solving
problems so great they cannot be named
even once we have reached our destination
and disembark into whatever weather
for a long time there is a compartment
within us filled with analog silence
inside us the dream goes on and on

## POEM FOR VOWS

*for E. and G.*

Hello beautiful talented
dark semi-optimists of June,
from far off I send my hopes
Brooklyn is sunny, and the ghost
of Whitman who loved everyone
is there to see you say what
can never be said, something like
partly I promise my whole life
to try to figure out what it means
to stand facing you under a tree,
and partly no matter how angry
I get I will always remember
we met before we were born,
it was in a village, someone
had just cast a spell, it was
in the park, snow everywhere,
we were slipping and laughing,
at last we knew the green secret,
we were sea turtles swimming
a long time together without
needing to breathe, we were
two hungry owls silently
hunting night, our terrible claws,
I don't want to sound like I know,
I'm just one who worries all night
about people in a lab watching
a storm in a glass terrarium
perform lethal ubiquity,
tiny black clouds make the final
ideogram above miniature lands

exactly resembling ours, what is
happening happens again,
they cannot stop it, they take off
their white coats, go outside,
look up and wonder, only we
who promise everything despite
everything can tell them
the solution, only we know.

## 3:14 P.M.

This blue pen I am holding

feels carved from a glacier so

my fingers are sad

which is a good way to begin

the me from 1998 says

to the me who of sadness

like everything is so tired

and the face of Nazim Hikmet

looks down he says

live like a squirrel

and the earth will someday

be an empty walnut maybe

with a little blue light

still in it like this pen

which was not carved but

made somewhere

I often wonder

whether anyone

from the kitchen where

we used to talk all night

about the freedom of the future

is still alive or have they all

like me gone into the business

of naming breezes

I named one sorrow magnet

and another dangerous agreement

like a tree I cried to the sun

I am your lost child of gold

but the sun said no

inch your way back

to the forest

in a thousand years

the shadows will tell you

who you were green one

## BIRDS OF TEXAS

I like to be alone in someone else's house,
practicing my cosmic long-distance wink.
I send it out toward a mirror
some distracted bored cosmonaut dropped
on an asteroid hurtling
closer to our star. No one watches
me watching thousands
of television hours, knitting
a golden bobcat out of
tiny golden threadlets. These good
lonely days every thing
I've claimed I've seen
for me to use it glows.
I'm waiting for the love
of Alice Ghostley, who keeps
in various faces and guises
appearing amid the plot machines,
always to someone more beautiful
and central in complex futile relation.
They call her plain but to me her name
sounds full of distant messages
beamed a thousand years ago,
only now to flower. Penultimate
cigarette, high desert breezes,
I've written all my plans and vows
on careful scraps of paper piled
beneath weirdly heavy little black rocks
I gathered on many slow walks
into town to ask no one who
would bother naming this particular
time between later afternoon
and twilight. Crazed bee, I know

the name of the plant you are in!
Salvia! Also, the jay is not blue,
nor the sky or indigo bunting,
within particles and feathers sun
gets lost making expert holographers
out of us all. Passarina, I saw
your dull blaze from the railing flash
and an insect disappeared. Afternoon
once again slipped into
the gas station like it did those old
days it had a body that moved
and smoked among the people,
whistling a cowboy song concerning
long shadows, happy and unfree.

## INTO THE ALPINE MEADOW I SEND A FEW SILENT DAWN APOLOGIES

She said last night she couldn't sleep
in the bed clearly designed
by someone who wanted to punish
future mothers for daring to lug
anyone into this terrible world.
And also the junior high school cheerleaders
staying at the hotel were so
truly happy it made her feel
the power of her inner murderous dowager.
Now it was quiet though still we felt
their martial cries echo with ominous
joyful sentience off the sides
of the mountains, melting the last
patches of early summer snow.
We were eating dinner outside
in that evening light that makes
everything familiar. In her hair Heather
wore a few little rose-colored flowers
as if to remind us she bears
with what we all agree is the grace
of the undeserving a most resonant name.
The question evening always poses
is who will be brave enough
to acknowledge our power to kindly order
the seneschal to walk down
the dark stairs into the cellar
for that supernumerary bottle of wine.
Someone's brother was saying
we should fret about a new interplanetary
radar capturing our messages
and placing them into facilities

full of black monoliths. In the dim light
another lit a candle, gathering our attention.
Little heliostar, something huge is coming.
Take my hand and we will go
into the new ceremony of acceptable forms
and with a single name make them ours
like the children of the dead we are.

## POEM FOR ANN HOOD

On my walk today
I heard behind
a wooden fence
someone sweeping
and thought on some
certain day I too
will have lived
long enough
to know the names
of what here
in Northern California
they call the seasons,
which music
makes the house
exactly happy
for no guests,
and how to wait
for a call from a far-
off happy child.
I looked up at three
crimson apples
from a single
high branch hung,
past them blue
endless steps
upward toward
whatever moved,
and to my beloved
morning glory
so purple at my feet
in Oakland everywhere
I said weed

that is a flower,
please tell me
can one grow
an orange bird
of paradise
in zone 9
so I can inform
my wife who loves
to place in the garden
what has a chance
to live with
more than a little
water and care.
It could not say.
Then in my mind
at last I thanked
you for the various
violet spectral
shades you so sweetly
joined to cover
the small new body
we wait to know.
All the while
you were knitting
you were surely
talking laughing
and as always thinking
also of something else,
and all became
amethyst midnight
wisteria nocturne
sound of jewels
and mourning
emperors to warm

ourselves beneath,
a little sad
and peaceful to know
I might not ever
know what time
is but you and I
have always been
sure it is nothing
like the carefully
draped resolved
or endlessly waiting
time in a book to which
we can always return.

## POEM FOR NOGUCHI

One morning I summoned the giant tome

it arrived by means so magical

I just put my open hand

down on it like a cloud

rests on the roof of a dark museum

full of stone teardrops

so smoothly carved they could not

have come from anywhere

but Obsidian Desert or an island

in the Emerald Sea he alone

by his dual nature could echolocate

if you go there visitor you will see

in those stones the reflection

of whatever about your shadow nature

you need to discover with unstable

certainty flicker while outside

the wells in the garden

forget dark attachments and remind

each other in the soft afternoon language

you are on an isthmus

like a hero from a novel

you have journeyed there by train

to become contemporary

as rare blue mountain flowers

other bodies are with you too

in a small dark room you are together watching

the same movie about his life

on a loop until the city

full of innovative playgrounds

he never built fills us

and again at last we are each

a child wandering this time happily alone

among the harmless shapes

that know whatever calm people know

## MY SABBATICAL

here in the provinces

no lights on

I regard the tall urn

plum flowers blooming

what is that rustling

oh it's my childhood

when I never said

you owe them nothing

in the darkness

of the skull

I have retired

on the veranda

it gets pretty quiet

poets are working

they say the night

we call

life is brief

tell me about it

a short nap then

their silent demands

that force

of cinnamon

rain has made

it cannot linger

people

for my own self

I feel loved

do I make

myself clear

Hawaii

why are you far away

and business

near my heart

thanks for the note

filled with violent homage

someone brands me

the river with no name

a person walking

looks small

people

what to give them

not so calmly

waiting together

a long time to die

## POEM FOR COLERIDGE

The lake was super fucking cold,
and with every smallest
increment got colder. I plunged
my head. Under no sound.
Not even extreme silentness.
No stupid ideas, no words
of comfort I should not
or not have not said, not my
constant horrible ungrateful
desire to have different form
or be done. All this talking.
Not even breath. Everyone
was really gone. There is no
word for that x. Under
it outwaits time. Later on shore
wrapped in a white towel and still
feeling ridiculous and also
a little secretly proud for having
so mortally scared myself
I would say some mystical
inexorable communion feeling
toward those ancient blue
waters pulled me, meaning
I had already forgotten, I was
as always already talking too much
to keep away something numberless.

## BEHAVE THYSELF

*for Jim Tate*

He used to love to walk around

the little town checking up

on nothing saying behave

thyself to squirrels outside

the bookstore then sitting

an hour or so in the chair

they called his when he

wasn't around

I want to tell you

something it took me

a long time

to write any poems

I was always pretending

I was talking to a tree

no echo in the wind

also he was a very private man

it was more like he

loved among

there was a sound

some afternoons

like a record needle being

picked up too quickly

we all said thunder

where the baby goat was crying

in the hills its mother

loved it very much

but with distance

one day from Ashfield

it would be forever

brought down into the valley

to do great things

like visit Jim

he gets up from reading

*Street of Crocodiles* or young

Slovenians to pet

its head then goes

back to waiting

for a name to arrive

## UNPACKING MY BOOKS

one hundred years after his death
who gets to be next to Apollinaire on the shelf
it wasn't even his real name
Bishop belongs next to Buson
her book a faded pink
every room I've ever lived in
was filled with exactly that light
thus my body too
as it recovered from sleep
and readied itself for the temporary
lower down Paul Celan
alone in an apartment he wrote
a final letter to Nelly Sachs
their words to each other
proximately sleep in a small brown book
they only met once
in a hotel named after a stork
later he wrote her gold
crossed the water toward them
then threw himself in the Seine
this was a difficult decision
mine had to be too
at last I knew it could only be
wild Corso interrupting
sanctimony with true holy
profane drunken moments
I look down to see
my finger still crooked from long ago
who does that infamous
hand belong to
say the innocent name
with it I try to match

the style of an ancient scroll
still buried yet audible
gripping nothing I find
the firm handshake of a surrealist
greeting us in the doorway
of a large ruined hotel
the sky the color of cognac
the war guttering temporarily out
leaving only those little fires
Auden wrote about
as always as if he were looking down
out of the corner of my eye
silver syntax glitters
Issa's little green year
Joshua told me to find
O transbluent flowers of evil
I thought Pessoa could handle Pound
every poet is still alive
full of wine shouting in the galleries
portraying sorrows of the world
Vasko Wisława Audre
wizards of sleep I'm waving at you
from psychological time
I can already smell the smoke
and know we won't just be different
soon it will be a winter for us
nuclear snow in the bitter headlights
in such hard times we grasp
for understanding poetry
we touch the bright star
but that dream eludes us
you are already gone
so we go on not knowing
what it is necessary to relinquish

## POEM FOR TOMAŽ ŠALAMUN

When I first got to know him
it was summer and all the poets had gone to the islands
so I followed behind on the train to Rijeka
then a boat moving farther south
I slept on the deck and very softly
with a mental plectrum played
Gregor's guitar like I was forgetting
one long wordless song
about night islands
in the morning I stumbled onto land
and walked two-thirds asleep
out onto some stone steps
leading downward and jumped
directly into several abandoned villages
and emerged in a lavender field
I had never seen so much perfect water
and so many beautiful people
all on mopeds moving so fast
I talked to not even one of them
in those days I was always traveling
every day was the saddest and greatest
I was completely free
the intense sun and radioactive pleasure
others were experiencing were slowly translating
me yet the essence still mysteriously inhered
many years later in a bar
in some eponymous town with sleepy hotels
I realized that he was that rare being
who could read the golden books
we only knew from the songs
our older brothers listened to
behind closed doors

and now it is always too late
also he was a historically terrible driver
especially up into mountains
probably because inside him
something else was always happening
what mystics call a third eye
opening onto sublime demon vistas
Rimbaud and Stevens and Plath saw too
I do not have a third eye
or at least it is only open at an uncertain
forsaken particular night
hour when in my total blindness
I know like a poet time
allowed to grow old falling in love
is no kind of death
and I understand at last
that was now and this is then

## STARI TRG

is the name
of the old square
where I sat
one afternoon
in pleasant castle
shadow drinking
tea with a few
mostly silent
young poets,
then consulted
a hand-drawn map
leading to your
new paintings,
dusk had been
for too long
next to the canal
lingering
and it was past
the moment
to walk to the opening
where whoever
everyone was
Tomaž had said
would be
to celebrate
your brilliant colors,
little green
dragon statues
on the bridge
watched me
from the table
rise and make

a strange
unpracticed wave
to Tone Primož
and Gregor who
I did not know
I already knew
were my brothers
then place my feet
exactly where
in that moment
I was wrong
to be sure
Vasko Popa
had once
stood thinking
*sentient deer,*
it sounds too strange
not to be true
but truly for several
minutes like
I was a trolley
and she was going
home from work
a mantis rode
my shoulder,
off she climbed
and I made
a left at the statue,
there was time,
I stood awhile,
the little square
had a kiosk,
I handed my money
through its window

for cigarettes
and a newspaper
I thought I would
somehow understand,
for when I was young
I had studied
the older sister
language to those
almost familiar words,
in those unconnected
days I walked
through the morning
past the sad kids
with colored hair
and the graves
of Amherst, their
old stern
uncomforting words
carved in stone
comforted me,
they said death
happened
a lot yet here
you go
on your way
to the Russian
to eat a little snow
knowledge chipped
from the vast,
grasping the paper
in the park
now too late
for the party
for the paintings,

I felt something
above me fly
with feathers
by, I was
holding a key,
if I made a left
night would grow
and if I walked
up the stairs
all those books
where nothing
happened would
happen to me,
I went straight
ahead toward
the mountains
always looking back,
and now Tomaž
is gone and so
is Jim and so
many others faster
than I can
write their names
which may be why
in your newest
paintings the figures
live under a translucent
substance holding
grey sand
like words hold
what they mean
but also are,
rabbit, skull,
that's a horse

looking at
a figure looking
back to say
I love you life
but I must go

*for Metka Krašovec*

## POEM WRITTEN WITH BUSON

He told us
to go outside

and if someone talked to us
to be silent

not in a hostile way
more like after the bells

have stopped
performing

more like the building
glazed with sun

no longer heard
in evening wind

he stumbles suddenly
it's because they have voted

to stop thinking
life can be taken away

girls from Ōhara
owls darkening

the maples at evening
I have never been

on a difficult journey
my beloved village

no longer satisfies me
the white flower

in the darkness of the heart
the gateway at midnight

someone goes through
to become invisible

in the capital
when the lanterns

of finance
have been extinguished

the two of them
whose love

is no longer new
feel strengthened

by wine and the songs
that make the path

that can only
be seen in darkness

hours later the rustling
of her robe

says an old well
is a frightening thing

## POEM FOR ÉLUARD

what clouds can teach us
in the capital of sadness

is the rose
is always public

and all houses are yellow
just sit in one

like a seamstress
longing for the longing

childhood was
put an orange on his grave

to thank him for lying
he left the war

in a train
toward the past

when sometimes
we were bored

he took off his hat
read his little

poems for peace
and was welcomed

into the fellowship
of productive dreaming

in the world
the woman

was also moving
so he gave his passport

to a desperate friend
then discovered

time overflows
I will never understand

I only know he
and his fellow travelers

would be so sad
to be here to discover

now there is no one
in the narrow corridors

who is not sold

## POEM ON THE OCCASION OF A WEEKLY STAFF MEETING

Across the deep eternal sky
a thousand changing shapes flit by,

i.e. clouds, or so I have always called them.
But how is it I have never

among my incessant coffee refills
and insectivorous travels

among the cubicles in search
of individual wrapped chocolates

and conversations asked you
if you in my heart detect

several as I do in yours
of the adorable qualities

of broken folding chairs?
Or why we build desired outcomes

on the spots where old ones stood?
I call this meeting to order:

item one let's go to lunch and order
wild boar. Let's have an old-world chat

about the original action items.
O fuck the fluting on the donuts!

I feel totally Anglo Saxon!
I want for once in my life to whip

around an actual halberd gleaming
in the sun and win

a great victory versus the air!
Here is my project update:

the file cabinet is watching
over the particles

safely asleep in a beam,
and nothing into our building

has at last so gently crashed
leaving us bored and fortunate.

I move our faces
around this highly polished table

to each other look
almost familiar

so let us slip into the light
blue sleeve this afternoon

so gracefully carries
the next few hours in

and together forget
what our great task is.

## SUMMER POEM #3

In the middle of my life I had the most marvelous piece of luck

I entered a hotel and among golfers pregnant

with beautiful minor worries watched

the cheerleaders gallop as James Wright said

terribly against each other's bodies

but really it was not except for their cries

of happiness bouncing off the mountains

surrounding us in the middle of my life

in the middle of my life I felt lost and awake

a patient who has just been told he has

fifty years to live his body a responsibility

now a machine that must like an animal

for some inexplicable reason be cared for

goodbye lassitude of adult childhood

on the ocean immense aggregated plastic floats

toward us and our most brilliant scientists

can only just watch it

*because* is such an interesting word

we must somehow figure out how to put people in it

## WHAT IS THE NATURALIST SAYING?

The chain saws make it hard to tell.
Golden mantis? Let's go
smell a tree? That can't be right.
But I go and dutifully press
my two-barreled pollen catcher
to the rough bark and say yes,
indeed, maple mixed with
a little cologne a jackass
dating your sister would wear.
Now he's into chipmunk tactics,
them watching each other
in the snow. Little black toenails.
Mutually assured nut destruction.
A mostly nocturnal mule's ear,
I drift in the useful wind.
With whatever the side
of the mountain that's winning
says I must agree. On sunny days
this I remember: I sure do love
my shadow more than I love
my mirror! The truth is I prefer
to be inside, silently visiting
a sick old hobbit irony
has not mastered. Some
jays are shy. I never knew!
Others will build
happily a nest in the spandrel
above the post office no one
enters anymore. Who even
writes letters? They are extinct,
like art you can't talk about
or Crypt Binaca. Now someone

from New Alabama is asking
a question exactly like she's
reading a manual just above
the naturalist's head. I can't hear
anything, the chain saws
are coming closer, the hobbit
is saying goodbye to a boring life,
but at least he never shaved his feet.
In just a few hours it will be noon
and our shadows beneath us
into tiny circles smaller than a pin
will disappear, but we won't know,
we'll be so deep inside summer
talking we've finally been forgotten.

## THE PRIVILEGE OF POETRY

Over someone's shoulder
I read we should listen
to everything

but the more I listen
the more my fingers are lonely
in the abandoned house

where the absence of music
is a kind of music
as the theorist whose name

I forgot wrote
and when I read it
it was so wrong

I gasped like all my thoughts
had been sucked out
into the ocean to crash

back in onto my head
where the shadow of a wasp
keeps arriving

if only I were truly willing
to have a little evil
poured into my ear

says the politician inside me
who will never win
I am almost

too busy to vote
it's just me on those days
I am trying to hear

the dark light of a terrarium
when it longs to be a park
buried underneath

pre-human snow
so I can tell you
which is the privilege of poetry

## ANOTHER SONG

my mild grandfather
Benjamin came
from the most
aristocratic poor,
they looked down
from a house
near a river
on everyone
and almost believed
they would not
along with the rest
be taken,
but one day they
like all the frightened
got on a boat
to the new land
where he grew up
in comfort and saw
everyone prosper,
then he married a dark
disapproved-of one
with an inherited
anger we too someday
would come to know,
right before I was
born he wrote a letter
to General Dynamics
asking for a job,
he was already what
they called old,
in the letter he said
he had delivered

messages full
of fate to generals,
huddled over serious
maps they stretched
out their hands without
looking and took
what he gave them,
it was always correct,
and now his only
daughter was having
a first son he
somehow knew
would never become
a master of industry,
born in shame
I am only sure
I know I don't ever
want to be paid,
I stand before
the certain flowers
of youth and pretend
to myself I believe
what I say when
all I want is to write
letters to everyone
and pin them
on the wind until
someone wiser
than me understands
how exactly things
must change,
I agree
and promise
I will put

whatever is queer
in my shoulder
to the infamous wheel,
but please don't
make me decide
what will happen
to the souls who
must be punished
and who should be
allowed to escape
with their sins
and make
the next world

## REVERSE TRUTH SONG

I'm so tired
of dirty water
the rich on their boats
old magic
when I get my money
like a corpse
I clasp myself
beneath the surface
where there are no rules
when I was younger
sometimes shaded
or bright with sun
I walked down streets
named after presidents
named after trees
I was eleven
I fell asleep in the library
saw her face
and never woke
since then she
has sometimes
appeared in people
I meet her
in their faces shining
like one who just
married another
each day my mouth
looks more like
a mouth about
to say something
that matters
like it's never good

to come home
not yet and you can't
see the planet
or leave your body
you can go to the lake
but no one cares
except the ones
who love you
they don't want
to harm you
but you always
need a name
or how will they find you

## TO THE BAY BRIDGE

I hate decoration
except on ancient fortresses
like the Alhambra
where many years ago
I took my darkness
but could not leave it
the blue tiles
were too bright
I loved them so
dazed in the hope
ok not right now
but maybe soon
life will become
less in the same
boring way interesting
out the gate I drifted
into narrow streets
that kept curving
always downward
until I turned
one final time
onto a street
and stood before
a little church
guarded by
a demon perched
above the door
forever to scare
the few believers
left into taking
shelter in the cool
shadows of weekly

mystification
I stood there
waiting for a solemn
diurnal ritual to end
so I could go inside
and touch the walls
and understand
as always nothing
I know it's probably
wrong to love
old movie theaters
in Midwestern towns
cluelessly resembling
an Arab palace
in the mind
of the vice president
of the rotary club
only a few faded
walls and minarets
remain surrounding
lions inside the lobby
nobly asleep in a slow
benevolent local
commerce dream
that business
once was young
here in the west
they finally built
the new bridge
across the bay
it glows in white
unadorned solicitude
as if it will never
become obsolete

driving across it
the electric buses
blink go warriors
in pure silent fog
and everyone agrees

## 4TH OF JULY

In the new town where we moved
to solve our very real problems
leaving our friends and neighbors behind
for strange potential
there is an old-timey parade
families in their neurotypical glory
gleam along the street on the highest hill
the one with the giant houses looking
down all the way to the water and the bridges
to the city where you work in the golden
light of imagining progress is possible
all the families cheer as restored old cars
drive by starting with the Model T
I had never seen one before
then the mayor riding in a convertible
throwing candy to the children
the parade is over everyone lines up
to eat hamburgers and listen to a band
it is fourth of July and this year
this project seems designed to fail
spectacularly taking all of us somewhere
we were destined from the first time
a new colorless race put its foot down
the ground trembled and now at last everyone
thinks they see this project is designed to fail
even the red white and blue star
knows there is no future in the hollow land
without reparation to those who were here
and those we brought but how to begin
is the only question left to ask
besides will capitalism die while
we are still alive or will it wait to be alone

## THE CRITIC

once had long hair
lots of curls
down to his shoulders
like Shelley
but without feelings
in his poems
this was long ago
when everyone
was a poet
sad and free
many wrote books
only a few
became great
not he
though he is
in a useful way
brilliant not unlike
a lighthouse
born to illuminate
our dangerous
mistaken attractions
to what we blindly
think we love
and thus
will destroy us
but not quite
enough to ask
why he feels
so strongly
he must tell us
what is wrong
with the work

of a young poet
born in a place
America calmly
poured liquid
fire onto
who grew up poor
and queer
until somehow
true miracle
poetry saved him
whose book
everyone reads
and weeps
and says at last
*poetry*
it must be lonely
to be the critic
at his desk
almost like a poet
sure he knows
something we have
all forgotten
the critic
reads the book
the lighthouse
penetrates
the gloom
to reveal
poems that only
safely pretend
to be as dangerous
as life
which is full
as everyone knows

of shitty undecorated
feelings that are
not like anything
but just sit
without substance
yet completely
palpable
on our shoulders
or chests
yes but what
is the use
in this storm cloud
of anger fear
and poison water
of being correct
about imperfect
things everyone loves
is the question
I am too tired
to answer
while we wait
for the next
terrible piece of news
I will tell you
a secret everyone
who knows
poets knows:
most of the time
poets are not
they are bureaucrats
counting counting
until drained
of all but desperation
they stumble

upon the symbol
and asleep
carry it back
to the poem
where their faces
can disappear
and finally
be forgotten
only then
can they escape
the precincts
of what keeps us
safely where
we are doomed
and write what
will not save us
but only begin

## ROSEANNE BARR

is there anyone worse
than Roseanne Barr?

she is the spear tip
of white resentment

her fake working-class
caustic humor

can be irresistible
as an opiate

you take to rebel
and become an accomplice

which makes laughing
a kind of fascism

when the time comes
someone should bury her

in the forest
like a mushroom

and put up a big sign
that says don't eat

this poisonous mother

## THE BLACK BIRD

I wrote a poem once
I thought it was to be
honest just ok
then it went "viral"
everyone loved it
and soon enough
I almost did too
though I also knew
something nameless
I pushed down
ever deeper
I wrote more
a whole book
named after
the viral poem
it won all the awards
people even
really named
a whole conference
after it and wept
when they even
thought about it
it was far too much
so extreme
it had to be real
what I had done
now whenever
I try to write
I feel so afraid
of feeling nothing
so I just write house
and war

and dapple
everyone smiles
and says yes
but really I just
want to get high
and sit on the porch
of my heart
(yes of my heart
that's what I said)
where I can watch
the city go by
and imagine buildings
have feelings
but whenever I close
my eyes and try
to go there I only
see a black bird
with a yellow beak
staring at me
I keep waiting
but it just stares
back at me
and does not speak
even one word
from the other world

# THE POETRY READING

At the poetry reading I am listening
to the endless introduction.
The young poet waits
for a cloud of applause
through which he will go
to his doom. But I am starting
to know it will never end,
it will go on for years, then
at last I will die. Then
at my reading in Hell
this same one in the black
eyeglasses with his zombie
theories will once again appear.
He will talk and it will never end
and then it will and I will
rise to stand before a dark
room full of baseball caps,
some even red, all turned
down toward lit phones.
I will look down at my papers
and open my mouth
to discover my voice all along
had the hint of plangent
mall jazz punctuated
by occasional appropriated
working-class pathos.
And together in the great
posthumous wooden hall
full of breathable poetic history
where so many others
with names we cannot forget
have read to the adoring,

together we shall with the help
of my poems reach at last
the inescapable conclusion
that poetry truly makes
nothing that is not already
sad happen, its time
that never came is over,
and no one who cares
even a little about the world
and its denizens can
justify whatever energy
writing it releases into
the already burning air.
We are all dying into
the afterlife of knowing
exactly what is important to say.
When this moment comes
I will be reading a poem
in which father was drunk,
reeking in the lamp
stolen from the sort of
fancy hotel I pretend
without a wince not to love.
Then in the poem jute orchids
and similes for darkness
shall manifest and dissolve
into proper names asleep
in the creepy presumption
of intimacy without compassion.
Painfully hilarious in its sad
failure this poem for an instant
in its absence of all holy matters
reminds me how once
in a green journal I wrote

along with the truth
of my love for R
which still remains
the promise I will not
whatever comes forget
to remember what it was like
to be thirteen. And then
I forgot. The audience
gasps at the first actual
thought. The claims
for poetry are too
extravagant and not
enough, poems don't belong
anywhere, and no matter  with what ardor we say
the rain is the rain N
and C will go on alone,
their tender love I watched
fiercely blossom
in my community has shattered
and will be buried like a crimson
Etruscan vase fringed
with the most gorgeous black.
And now each stanza
in the crazed mirror
of the obsolete lyric
will reflect a different era
in what I am forced to call my life.
The first will describe
the years I was too smart
to write anything,
when the productive cruelty
of my parents forged me
into the applicant. Then

the decade I played too many
and not enough notes.
The month in the brownstone
with the widow and her
desperate suits that hung
on my body I took fatherless
to the matinee. I got married
and had a child, so the hidden
subject of money would
no longer cease
in the cognizant shadows
to lurk. The poem will end
with the days
of the doomed nozzle
and other unmentionable
devices that saved
and therefore condemned us.
And then the appearance
of the Omega. And every time
a black sun gets mentioned
another demon sobs.
Just one more short lyric
and then we can go
drink our goblets of blood.
This one is called The Crooked Hotel,
it's about a vacation
where all the truths were traced
back to their original sorrows.
It ended in a cloistered
nostalgia for the present
she and I called ours, and our
mild happy tears coursed
down and watered

the garden we walked
until the end of our days
that came too soon.

## GENERATION X

I was born the autumn
after a wave of flowers
swept the land

too late to appear in even
one poem by Frank O'Hara
so my poems do not delight me

which until recently
I didn't even realize
was an option

I always just hoped
at best they could be
good-natured rebellious

first sons who wander
intently curious but
not too brilliant

as if Wordsworth scrubbed
of self-regard got drunk
on a Greek island

with L. Cohen and Marianne
then they all went to see
Emily putting on

a black dress to go out
and meet her dangerous love
under an arbor of stars

crying blood and nameless
birds with black eyes
that attack everyone

so she could not hang out
but gave them the other dress
I have always been afraid

to wear and some drugs too
and they took them and went
to a library and cried

then the intercom informs
the kids there is no threat
after all and rising up

from behind their desks
they reach out
with strange smiles

dear committee of the future
I could tell you I am almost
sure you will find my poems

unacceptable because
they appropriate the common
human experiences of fear

and desire taking little
sips from the nest
dumping bits of blue

into the river which until
my poems was more
than cerulean enough

but the truth is
I want you and everyone
to like them

so I sit up here born
too early and late
staring at these trees

their black leaves turning
slowly dull green
in the morning light of tasks

ashamed I actually open
my mouth to ask
mundane diurnal silence

to help me forget
whatever I know
so I can write

what I am sure
people will mostly
not read or tell me

no matter how clearly
I speak they sorrowfully
don't understand

then I switch on the hum
of my old device to listen
to the sons of no one

sing and remember
yes because I belong
to the first generation

that named itself
my great ambition has
always been to be

a loser with pointless integrity
that just serves the man
and with the fatal certainty

of the most useless
letter in the alphabet I know
to say who cares we've got

Kim Gordon and Deal
and these cigarettes
will just kill someone else

and there's always a job
for people who sort of
studied the quadrivium

and at least when we are
kissing their asses
we know it's wrong so

lovingly not forgiving
ourselves for hating ourselves
is the only solution

## POEM FOR HARM

Walt Whitman
you cannot know

how a live oak feels
much less a woman

or anyone sold
does it help

to think that way
to wander

into everyone's experience
with love you told yourself

and therefore believed
was innocent

to break off a twig
and bring it back to your room

then write
by its harmless light

to listen to you
has helped me

in dark times
and when you said

you were like the grass
a uniform hieroglyphic

growing with equal
distant affection

"among black folks
as among white"

I believed you
your whole life you made

one book some people
now take out into the forest

to ritually burn
because elsewhere you wrote

when you were more than
old enough to know

what you truly thought
of the intellect

of black folks who
were not inside your song

Walt Whitman
should your words

here be said
in pain and shame

or left for only dead wind
to hear

if we keep it
like a secret does its dark

force grow
for my whole life

I thought words
could not harm

I too looked down
but then I had a son

about whom people say
what even I once said

Walt Whitman you are still
my favorite poet sometimes

but what poison
can you drink and live

is the question I ask
in the few moments I have

before my son
lying in bed singing

about feeling like a volcano
slams open the door

and demands
of everyone to be loved

## ASTROLOGY

Dottie I hate astrology
and the way you sit there
you and Bianca
looking down on my poems
I can almost hear you thinking
how did he get so old
why did we ever pretend
we liked to listen to
his various hues of darkness
and occasional pale glows
this is projection I know
I know you are full
of true love for poetry
made not just by yourself
and for that I really do love you
also I adore your earrings
the little toy fruits and plates
and your brilliant
terrifying mind
but the way you look down
even though you do not
with the mystics on me
destroys me
Dottie you are a green jewel
a scary green jewel
that can tell the future
so much better than astrology
which is really stupid
though no birds get killed
so I guess it's harmless
unless you let it direct you
but then again

Dottie your last book
made me afraid to be a mother
I add it to all the others
the real fears about my son
I will tell you sometime
how different he is
it causes me to marvel
even when I feel the fears
I imagine them
in some part of my mind
let us not call it the library
let us call it the door
Dottie your poems
make me want to open it
for a long time now truth
has been a ridiculous word
for what power guides
my mind half asleep
pushing me further
where I am so afraid to go
Dottie you have seen my chart
so you know I was born
on the terrible cusp
of reason and dream
and there I will always remain
waving at you as you pass
in your green craft
knowing you will return

## MY DOG

*for Eileen Myles*

Away from joy
you walk a little
missing a tooth
discussing famous
black dogs
on the dead
chests of lovers
I just finally
heard
that unnoticed
silence
of never having
one again
it's been with me
all my life
I saw mine
named after
a god
his body laid
out on the lawn
brown fur
dried blood
yes it's wise pathos
this want to live
in my body
like a dog
not thinking
if stones
for human deaths
then what
for the other ones

## THE PLEDGE

yesterday I kicked a tree
a walnut fell in a grave
nobody got hurt

it's June
the February
of summer

alone in Oakland
cleaning white ash
from not so distant fires

off my windshield
with my sleeve
I think of you

far old friend
scribbling poems
in the park

to your wife
and saying them
happily to no one

do you remember
when we pledged
to always look?

we were sadder
than Chinese poets
of the Northern Song

like them
in desperate times
we drank a lake

sized amout of wine
which made us strong
because we knew

no matter how much
everything matters
our poems can always

be read by anyone

## A LOVE SONG

I lie here next to you
thinking of you

frost at midnight
in my heart

there is no light

is it anger
or is it need

you far off there
probably dreaming

you married
someone
you never met

I don't want
to look like him

so I put on my shoes
each day
and lumber
out the black door

scaring the lake

Emily Dickinson
once said why
she never married

no one listened

she was always
far away

like England
where I've never been

why did you say
I love you but

it's true
there's a blue tower
in my mind

away from you
where I must go

## PENULTIMATE POEM

Let us walk one more time very slowly
to the famous meadow whose name eludes us
from there we can see the ghost ship
sail off the lake and into the clouds
let's speculate on where it has gone
and touch the glass thought animals and talk
about the machine that makes nothing matter
so totally it will never be different
our lives have already changed
and now we all have to go
back into the city and combine
pleasurably or at least well with the day
we will walk beneath the huge blue
gorgeous corporate windows and know
they are glass cases the figurines
inside them so carefully painted
they are almost completely alive
like our parents under the earth
their low voices in the kitchen say
they didn't mean anything by it and now
like great dead poets they understand us
just one more thing no matter how long
it seems it has been gone this feeling
everything you touch with your mind
so beautifully together belongs
will keep falling up into your life
like airplanes rise into the miraculous
unremarkable sky over the harbor
and its great ships taking their names out to sea

## I COMMIT

I commit to vote because
I'm pretty sure I grab
whatever I need from the world
and place it in my mind
which is getting incrementally
like the commons
undeniably more toxic and sad
yes I too walk around
considering my intractable problems
complaining it's too late
for more sonatas
everything is already too beautiful
music and anger won't save us
yet I commit to talking
earnestly with Sarah
about the school board
it will be night and we will be sitting
shoulder to shoulder
at the old table we love
each holding a pencil
like grade school children left alone at last
then in the morning
before our son wakes
I commit to holding
this tiny bit of quicksilver
(quick in the sense of living
in its very molecular nature
it wants to usefully combine with yours)
in my palm and to walking
up to the blue mailbox
I pass most mornings

in that familiar silence
under those nameless little trees
when all things that surround me wait

## ANOTHER POEM FOR ÉLUARD

thank you again
for the photograph
of his grave
he who said
the earth is blue
like an orange
which for an instant
seems precisely
correct because
it will always
be a solution
just out of reach
like that dream
you're in the forest
and you know
always deeper
is the way
then my son
wakes up too early
and bangs
the door
my intense anger
activates the hallway
and I feel
rug despair
then that flood
of adoration
while he munches
his toast
staring at music
without remorse

later my bored
eyes pass over
a thread informing
us poems are essays
oh yes exactly
as everyone
redelivers the endless
lecture on how
after much reflection
upon the flaws
of others we have
become marginally
less white
congratulations to us
our blankets
are not totally diseased
here take them
you don't have to thank us
we will humbly
accept the praise
our innocence
makes us free
of the stain
we massacred
basically everyone
and we're still here
to finish the job
thank you so much
for letting us forget
the only thing
we could do is buy
all the land
with our righteous

self-regarding sorrow
then give it back
and beg to stay
then leave anyway

## POEM FOR SANDRA

Sandra why did you try
to pay someone in some
water park in Georgia
with your faded socialist
pastel bills you brought
back from Greece
where deeper into your novel
and what we call love
you traveled
I guess you still hope
the end of money
could save the world
I've never seen
that famous sea
you were near
the one all those lost
cultures we mostly know
from remnants cross
in the book
I read each year
with the bored youth
of America
you have to teach them too
to you they come in
from the blazing sun
you cannot stand
and read
their boring poems
about how their world is ruined
it is but I like it
today because I can talk

to no one
in the dawn which I guess
you could say has grey fingers
like a dignified widow
surreptitiously touching
those trees
I bet you drank
a lot of retsina
the taste of pine
and the old sea
Sandra
stop hurting America
with your faceless
socialist money
if you don't stop
soon everyone
will feel sentient affection
and like the dream of Europe
we won't hate anyone
we will cry
and say farewell
to the cedars of Lebanon
I read today
at last they are dying
those great trees
that watched the humans
finally defeat the gods
that guarded them
so the Phoenicians
could be free at last
to use that tall wood
for long ships
that brought their purple

eponymous cloth
to the few
and alphabet to everyone

## MOVING DAY

goodbye yellow house
you used to be
down by the lake
where they built you
until they dragged
you up where it's dry
many years later
we came
with our happiness
terror and loss
we loved you so much
sometimes we pressed
our laughing faces
to your walls
and even kissed
them to thank you
it's silly to ask
who will we be
now that we're gone
into this new
place that still
echoes with
the steps of others
one day we too
will leave and what
are now strange trees
that do not know me
will have become
almost familiar
I will have asked them
so many times
help me forget

so I can survive
what little I know
about the way
happy child
his mind is made
of rooms where he goes
away from us
and everyone
and then returns
to be silent with his
remembered music
I can almost hear

## PHANTOM

in the early 1800s
poets walked for days
talking to each other
pouring significance
into the names
of what they saw
*lake sky nightingale*
*mountain forest*
*grasses darkness*
*ether gold sea*
saying them now
I sense natural power
and how it must
have felt to place
them so exactly
a spell that worked
now they hardly
mean anything
or too much
one word always
quietly resisted
light on water
it just reflected
everything that tried
to make it more
than what it was
it hasn't really changed
since it was said
by the Greeks
and even now
when it's spoken
it eludes

we still shudder
hidden soul that's near
form blended
into what surrounds
speaking it
can make you forget
your love of anything
and travel
into the past
such a relief
no matter how bad
it's over now
but I come back
each time to remember
this is not a story
and all things I love
are real and can
I don't want to write it
be destroyed

## POEM FOR MERWIN

for a long time you planted one every day
and now the garden is a clock on forest time

forest time where we were happy
for a few translucent hours moving
into the ghost houses
no longer there

and the shade houses
that are
their myth of air

and the places where people used to gather
by the stream that is now a dry bed
to eat and sing
we cannot almost hear them

then out along the narrow paths
over stones I kept forgetting
like years you had placed

and the dead clock face painters
covered in radium could not convey
their messages to us
here in the permanent shade

the palms with their very different leaves
and seed pods seem to say

you who think nothing can be repaired

you who will not ever
be able to describe our shapes
and say I love to no one

or today I was born

you burned astronomers
look at our wet leaves
maybe you were not even born
for knowing your own planets

you were not born for knowing
but saying

a piece of wood burned next to the little jade statue
means no matter how many times we leave
we will keep returning

it means no matter how many times we go
out where they sell executions

we will come back here
where the black gravestone
is a window in love with the beloved

on it is written here we were happy
which is true

reading it I would like to remember
what I am feeling now
that I would like not to be
the mechanism

a blade angled in reason

I too would like to lie down
in my own sort of field
green with potential love

today I know I was born
to try to remember
the name of the simplest leaf

from the tree of my childhood

I have always known that god all along

and that we were each born
the shadow of reality upon us

so be not easily angry
pick up the small rose book
with its disappearing house on the cover

enter its doorway
get lost for a while

forget we were born to carry our names

until it is our turn with nothing to say
except maybe we were born to love

and move further on

## TUNNEL PARK

eighty years ago
during those
famous dark times

when the government
paid men to build
bridges and dams

they carved this park
my son loves
out of a hill

the men needed
to keep working
to get paid

so they made
a long dangerous concrete
slide kids scream

down their parents
watching with
their hands

over their mouths
then dug
this unnecessary

cool aperture
full of obscure
shadows through

the hillside
to the garden
of famous roses

I don't care about
and finally some
secret stairs

no matter how many
times we have found
always seem

like they were
forever waiting
only for us

my son and I
went upward
his red shirt

kept disappearing
into the shadows
I became tired

from pointless worry
so we sat on
one stone step

and shared
some blue water
through the leaves

we could see
a giant crumbling
pastel house

it once was grand
its dark windows
still look down

on everything
it was so quiet
I could hear

the message
everyone knows
worse times

are coming
who isn't afraid
only the dead

we went farther
the stairs never ended
we had to turn

back to our lives
knowing there is
mystery even

in the new world

## AFTERWORD: LATE HUMANISM

In autumn 2016, I was in the slow midst of writing this book. Looking back, I can see a lot of personal and public dread in the poems I had already written, as well as in the writings of so many others. When our public life exploded that November, it felt like a calamity, but in retrospect it should have been predictable. It seems clear it was less an event than a revelation of what has been there all along, obvious to anyone who was simply looking.

In "A Defence of Poetry," Shelley wrote, "Poets are the hierophants of an unapprehended inspiration; the mirrors of the gigantic shadows which futurity casts upon the present." A century later, Spanish poet and Nobel Laureate Vicente Aleixandre deepened this idea, writing that the poet "is always one who reveals. The poet is essentially the seer, the prophet. But his 'prediction' is not a prediction of the future; it might well be of the past: it is timeless prophecy."

I love and fear the idea of poems as mirrors held to the past, the present, and even to the possible future. In those mirrors is revealed what Virginia Woolf calls "moments of being," when the "cotton wool" of ordinary existence is suddenly pierced or blown away. It is painful and hopeful. We are left with the immanence of our own existence, realizations heretofore hidden to us by others or ourselves.

A few weeks after the election, in December 2016, our son was diagnosed as being on the autism spectrum. It still feels a bit unreal to type those words, as if it is happening to someone else. For a while, in the spring of that next year, I didn't really write. Sarah and I were too busy trying to figure out what to do to help him, as he moved into his early school years. We were going to our jobs and doing all the daily things, and also trying to process and learn.

It turned out that I knew virtually nothing about autism, and what I did know was wrong. I thought of it as a disaster. All I had available to me were a few scattered, exaggerated characters in film and television, and incorrect facts. I didn't understand anything about why neurodiverse kids and adults react differently to the world around them, and how pervasive our negative stereotypes and assumptions are about this large, heterogeneous group. I had a lot to learn, about autism in general, and about my son in particular, and still do.

I was also made painfully aware that despite my own superficial iconoclasm and rejection of typical paths for my social class, I was deeply invested in traditional markers of success and conformity. To my shame, as well as my ongoing gratitude, my son's differences from expected norms initially threatened, then thankfully shattered, those anachronistic notions, in favor of the start of a much more loving and accepting attitude.

Starting later in 2017 and through the summer of 2018, I slowly started to write again. These new poems were of course filled with my emotions and thoughts both about my life as a father and as a stunned and horrified citizen. Without being specific, I mention my son's "diagnosis" (if that word is even appropriate, which, to the extent it carries within it the presumption of illness, I am sure it is not) in several poems, such as "My Life." This poem and others were written relatively early in the process of understanding how he is different, after the initial shock, but still in a time of great distress and ignorance. And yet, because of that distress, there is something profoundly true about the feelings in them.

I am not interested, here at least, in writing a memoir about autism or anything else. For one thing, the poems in this book obviously are concerned with many more things other than my son. Also, I am not trying to produce autobiographically generated sympathy or understanding. I am in search of different forces.

Virginia Woolf writes in "How Should One Read a Book?" about the difference between poetry and prose:

> The impact of poetry is so hard and direct
> that for the moment there is no other
> sensation except that of the poem itself.
> What profound depths we visit then — how
> sudden and complete is our immersion!
> There is nothing here to catch hold of;
> nothing to stay us in our flight. . . . The poet
> is always our contemporary.

How can a poet from a different time, place, background, cultural history be our "contemporary"? So much of what makes art interesting and human are its particulars. Everyone comes from somewhere, in time and place, and it is both inane and gross to pretend that this does not matter, when it matters more than almost anything. And yet, as Aleixandre writes, "Love, sorrow, hatred, death are changeless." This too seems true to me. I suppose this makes me, like Aleixandre, an old-fashioned humanist, which means I believe that even taking into account our very real, essential differences, the basic truths of human existence belong to all of us.

Those common truths are located in our languages and in our awareness. They appear in recurring symbols and myths, and also emerge from the everyday and the ordinary and the particular. Poets stumble upon them and reveal them, again and again. They are the source of the commonality that we find in the specifics of poetry, what makes every poet the contemporary of everyone, a friend. "What is it then between us?" asks Whitman in "Crossing Brooklyn Ferry." "It is not upon you alone the dark patches fall, / The dark threw its patches down upon me also."

Like language itself, every poem contains at least
the flicker of the individual imagination, while somehow,
paradoxically, offering the possibility of communion. Without
this possibility, the hope that we might find our way past
whatever separates us and remember we belong to the earth
and must together act to save it, it is no exaggeration to say
that as a species we are doomed.

I once heard the poet Mary Ruefle describe the difference
between poetry and fiction. Reading fiction, she said, we
remember the stories our parents told us at bedtime. In poetry,
we hear the songs they sung to us as we fell asleep. These are,
of course, not the same songs and stories for everyone, thank
god. But I am sure everyone longs for that experience, to be
sung to again or, if they never were, for the first time. To be
sung to is familiar and comforting and funny and sad and
eternal and full of mortal time, which is why everyone loves
poetry, whether they know it or not.

The book touches on many other things besides my son,
though his presence is everywhere in it. The struggle to truly
accept difference, and responsibility, and to move through real
fear and resistance to new understanding, is just as apparent to
me in our public life as in my private one, and each feels to me
like a reflection of the other, and therefore they are together in
this book.

My son of course is not a symbol, or a myth, nor, for
that matter, a diagnosis. In these poems, it is not he but my
image of him, animated by my hope and terror and love, that
becomes a symbol. I hope that is okay with him, and that
whenever he is old enough to read this, he will understand
why it was impossible for me to be a poet and write the truth
without including those feelings. I hope he will know that I
realize my fear was my own problem. It was something for me
to get through so I could see what has always been possible. I

can also see now that the hope and understanding I feel more each day were already revealing themselves in the poems. I just needed to catch up.

I never stopped seeing my son as the cheerful, lovely, clever, affectionate, funny, enthusiastic person he has always been, full of his own potential, to be revealed; stay tuned, everyone. I just got very afraid about his future, as I often am for our collective one. And hopeful too, and scared again, and so on. Most people can relate to that, I think, as parents or as citizens or something else. It seems many of us are struggling to understand ourselves as well as these days, as we must, if we choose not to be asleep.

January 24, 2019

## NOTES

"Stari Trg": The "Old Square" in Ljubljana, Slovenia, is famous for its Tea House, where the great Slovenian poets Gregor Podlogar, Tone Škrjanec, Primož Čučnik, and others often could be found. The painter Metka Krašovec was the wife of poet Tomaž Šalamun.

"Poem Written with Buson" was composed using a process for collaborating with the dead, invented by the poet Matt Rohrer.

The first two lines of "Poem on the Occasion of a Weekly Staff Meeting" are taken, for reasons now obscure to me, from "A poem on the occasion of the consecration of Sandford and Shippon Churches," published in 1855, by Rev. F. Wilson Kittermaster.

"Poem for Harm": In 1874, opposing the expansion of suffrage, Whitman wrote:

As if we had not strained the voting and digestive calibre of American Democracy to the utmost for the last fifty years with the millions of ignorant foreigners, we have now infused a powerful percentage of blacks, with about as much intellect and calibre (in the mass) as so many baboons. (*Prose Works 1892*, vol. 2, 762).

The phrase "keep it / like a secret" comes from the title of a record by Built to Spill.

"Poem for Merwin" was written after a visit to W.S. Merwin's home and surrounding palm preserve, in Ha'ikū, in Pe'ahi Valley on the north shore of Maui, Hawaii. According to the website of the Merwin Conservancy,

Over the span of nearly forty years, Merwin built an ecologically conscious home for himself and his wife Paula and planted more than 3,000 trees representing over 400 species of endemic, indigenous and endangered palms. He has transformed a place that was once considered "wasteland" into a lush and rare 19-acre tropical palm forest that is now considered one of the most important assemblages of palms in the world.

## ACKNOWLEDGMENTS

My love and gratitude to Sarah Karlinsky and the rest of my immediate and extended family, especially my sister Alexandra, my brother Michael, their families, and my mother, Marjorie. For their friendship and support, so much thanks to Rob Casper, Joshua Beckman, Noelle Kocot, Anthony McCann, Tod Goldberg, Charlie Wright, Heidi Broadhead, Ellen Welcker, Brenda Hillman, Leni Zumas, Daniel Handler, Bill Clegg, and Michael Taeckens. Especial thanks to Deborah Landau, Matt Rohrer, Srikanth Reddy, Robert Hass, Travis Nichols, Steve Almond, Ada Limón, Catherine Barnett, and Michael Wiegers, for reading many drafts and being so patient and kind and smart.

Great thanks and appreciation to the editors of the following publications, where these poems first were published: *The American Poetry Review, The Awl, Bat City Review, Fourteen Hills, jubilat, Love's Executive Order, Mānoa, McSweeney's, The National, The New Yorker, The New York Review of Books, Oxford Poetry, The Paris Review, Ploughshares,* Poem-a-Day, *Poetry, PoetryNow, A Public Space, Tin House,* and *Zyzzyva.*

"When I Was Fifteen" appeared in 826 Valencia's anniversary publication, *Fifteen.* "December" appeared in the *Boston Review* chapbook *Poems for Political Disaster.* "I Commit" was published as part of the McSweeney's Internet Tendency series *One Small Blow Against Encroaching Totalitarianism.* "Stari Trg" was written for an anthology dedicated to the work of Slovenian painter Metka Krašovec, *The Heart's Many Doors.* "I Wake Up before the Machine" was reprinted on PBS.org. "Poem for Vows" was reprinted in *Best American Poetry 2017.*

## ABOUT THE AUTHOR

Matthew Zapruder is the author of five collections of poetry, including *Come On All You Ghosts,* a New York Times Notable Book of the Year, and a book of prose, *Why Poetry.* He has received a Guggenheim Fellowship, the William Carlos Williams Award, the May Sarton Award, and a Lannan Foundation Residency Fellowship. His poetry has been adapted and performed at Carnegie Hall by composer Gabriel Kahane and Brooklyn Rider, and was the libretto for *Vespers for a New Dark Age,* a piece by composer Missy Mazzoli commissioned by Carnegie Hall for the 2014 Ecstatic Music Festival. He was the founding director of the Bagley Wright Lecture Series, and from 2016–17 he held the annually rotating position of Poetry Editor for the *New York Times Magazine.* He is an associate professor at Saint Mary's College of California, and editor at large at Wave Books.

Poetry is vital to language and living. Since 1972, Copper Canyon Press has published extraordinary poetry from around the world to engage the imaginations and intellects of readers, writers, booksellers, librarians, teachers, students, and donors.

WE ARE GRATEFUL FOR THE MAJOR SUPPORT PROVIDED BY:

THE PAUL G. ALLEN
FAMILY FOUNDATION

4
CULTURE

Anonymous
Jill Baker and Jeffrey Bishop
Anne and Geoffrey Barker
Donna and Matt Bellew
John Branch
Diana Broze
The Beatrice R. and Joseph A. Coleman Foundation Inc.
The Currie Family Fund
Laurie and Oskar Eustis
Mimi Gardner Gates
Nancy Gifford
Gull Industries Inc. on behalf of William True
The Trust of Warren A. Gummow
Carolyn and Robert Hedin
Bruce Kahn
Phil Kovacevich and Eric Wechsler
Lakeside Industries Inc.
on behalf of Jeanne Marie Lee

TO LEARN MORE ABOUT UNDERWRITING
COPPER CANYON PRESS TITLES,
PLEASE CALL 360-385-4925 EXT. 103

WE ARE GRATEFUL FOR THE MAJOR SUPPORT PROVIDED BY:

Maureen Lee and Mark Busto
Peter Lewis
Ellie Mathews and Carl Youngmann as The North Press
Hank Meijer
Gregg Orr
Petunia Charitable Fund and adviser Elizabeth Hebert
Gay Phinny
Suzie Rapp and Mark Hamilton
Emily and Dan Raymond
Jill and Bill Ruckelshaus
Cynthia Sears
Kim and Jeff Seely
Richard Swank
Dan Waggoner
Barbara and Charles Wright
Caleb Young as C. Young Creative
The dedicated interns and faithful volunteers
of Copper Canyon Press

# Lannan Literary Selections

For two decades Lannan Foundation has supported the publication and distribution of exceptional literary works. Copper Canyon Press gratefully acknowledges their support.

### LANNAN LITERARY SELECTIONS 2019

Jericho Brown, *The Tradition*

Deborah Landau, *Soft Targets*

Paisley Rekdal, *Nightingale*

Natalie Scenters-Zapico, *Lima :: Limón*

Matthew Zapruder, *Father's Day*

### RECENT LANNAN LITERARY SELECTIONS FROM COPPER CANYON PRESS

Sherwin Bitsui, *Dissolve*

Marianne Boruch, *Cadaver, Speak*

John Freeman, *Maps*

Jenny George, *The Dream of Reason*

Ha Jin, *A Distant Center*

Deborah Landau, *The Uses of the Body*

Maurice Manning, *One Man's Dark*

Rachel McKibbens, *blud*

W.S. Merwin, *The Lice*

Aimee Nezhukumatathil, *Oceanic*

Camille Rankine, *Incorrect Merciful Impulses*

Paisley Rekdal, *Imaginary Vessels*

Brenda Shaughnessy, *So Much Synth*

Frank Stanford, *What About This: Collected Poems of Frank Stanford*

Ocean Vuong, *Night Sky with Exit Wounds*

C.D. Wright, *Casting Deep Shade*

Javier Zamora, *Unaccompanied*

Ghassan Zaqtan (translated by Fady Joudah), *The Silence That Remains*

The poems are set in Dante.
Book design and composition by Phil Kovacevich.